THE LITTLE MUSLIM BOOK OF PRAYERS

A Green Fig Book

Illustrated by Yara Mahdi

Name:

Dear Parents and Teachers

The five prayers are among the best acts of worship that Muslims perform. Performing them is the best deed after having the correct belief in God and His messenger. The Prophet, may peace be upon him, was asked about the best deed; he said "الصلاة لوقتها" which means: performing the obligatory prayers at the beginning of their time (narrated by al-Bayhaqiyy).

Green Fig is happy to present the first book in the prayer series *The Little Muslim Book of Prayers*. It teaches very young children the names of the five obligatory prayers with captivating illustrations and rhyming sentences that will help the child memorize the names of the five prayers and set the foundation for a more detailed description of the prayers and their times. When a child reaches the age of mental discrimination, called in Arabic *tamyeez*, it is incumbent on the guardian to teach him how to pray and wake him up from time to time to perform the Dawn prayer so he will get used to doing so. If those aforementioned matters are neglected, the guardian would be sinful. The child himself is not accountable and no sins are written on him. However, the child who has reached the age of *tamyeez*, acquires reward for the good deeds he does, like prayer. Previous Muslim nations also had prayers obligated on them. All Prophets came with one religion, Islam - but the number of prayers was different. For example, only one prayer was obligated at the time of Prophet Adam, the first prophet.

We encourage you to draw your child's attention to the call of prayer every-time it is called from the minarets, or when you call the prayer at home prior to praying. Furthermore, let the child always perform the five prayers in congregation with you. This will instill in his heart the love and importance of the five prayers, so that he will be keen to perform them properly when it becomes due on him.

We hope that you will enjoy reading this book with your child at home or in the classroom. We would love to hear from you at info@greenfigbooks.com.

Green Fig Staff

Before sunrise it is the dawn
I peek outside and see a fawn

When the sun moves to the middle of the sky

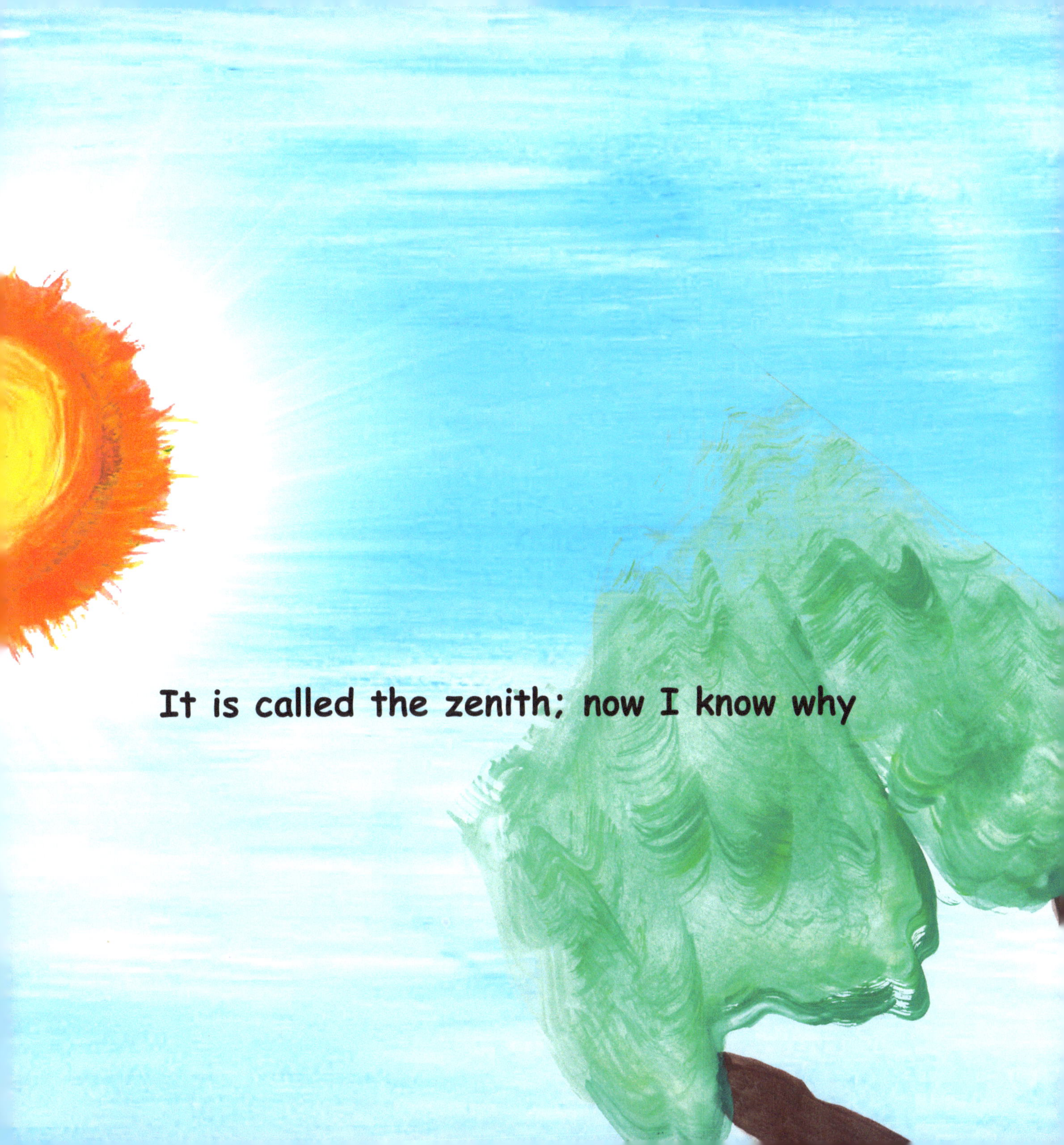

It is called the zenith; now I know why

Then the sun moves
This prayer time's "noon"
Look high in the sky
Wow! A balloon!

My shadow is long in the afternoon
Time to go back inside soon

The night starts at sunset
I hear the adhan from the minaret

Many small stars in the night sky appear
Nightfall prayer, we end our day here

Make wudu', go and pray
We do this five times a day

Dawn, noon, afternoon, sunset, and nightfall

Are the names of the five
prayers, and I love them all !

There are

5

FIVE

PRAYERS

each day and night

الله أكبر الله أكبر....

Adh-dhuhr

الظهر

The NOON Prayer

Al-'Asr

العصر

The AFTERNOON Prayer

Al-Maghrib

المَغْرِب

The SUNSET Prayer

Al-'Ishā´

العشاء

The NIGHTFALL Prayer

Al-Fajr

الفَجْرُ

The DAWN Prayer

When it's time for prayer
Muslims call the adhan

الله أكبر الله أكبر...

Allāhu Akbar Allāhu Akbar...

(God is the greatest God is the greatest...)

It means:

God is the most powerful,
God is the most knowledgeable,
no one can prevent what He has willed.

Encourage your child or student to memorize
the ḥadith of the Prophet:

_____

«بُنِيَ الإِسْلَامُ عَلَى خَمْسٍ: شَهَادَةِ أَنْ لَا إِلَهَ إِلَّا اللَّهُ وَأَنَّ مُحَمَّدًا رَسُولُ اللَّهِ،
وَإِقَامِ الصَّلَاةِ، وَإِيتَاءِ الزَّكَاةِ، وَحَجِّ البَيْتِ، وَصَوْمِ رَمَضَانَ.»
رواه البخاريّ ومسلم.

"Islam is based on five matters:
Testifying no one is God except Allāh
and that Muḥammad is the Messenger of Allāh,
performing the prayers, paying Zakah,
performing Pilgrimage and fasting Ramaḍān."
Narrated by al-Bukhāriyy and Muslim.

Proud Muslim Kids

The Proud Muslim Kids series by Green Fig books is designed to engagingly teach youngsters basic concepts of Islam in a way that speaks to their hearts and minds. Each book in the series is crafted by a staff of qualified educators, writers, illustrators, parents and children. Not only is the Proud Muslim Kids series designed to supplement the early childhood and elementary Islamic curriculum, it is a great addition to any school or home library. Covering a wide variety of topics such as the Five Pillars of Islam, Islamic culture, and Islamic history, parents and children will return to these books and enjoy them together time and time again.

Green Fig

www.ingramcontent.com/pod-product-compliance
Lightning Source LLC
Chambersburg PA
CBHW040230070426
42447CB00030B/90